How to Write
Writing Poetry

by Nick Rebman

FOCUS READERS®
BEACON

www.focusreaders.com

Copyright © 2024 by Focus Readers®, Mendota Heights, MN 55120. All rights reserved. No part of this book may be reproduced or utilized in any form or by any means without written permission from the publisher.

Focus Readers is distributed by North Star Editions:
sales@northstareditions.com | 888-417-0195

Produced for Focus Readers by Red Line Editorial.

Photographs ©: Shutterstock Images, cover, 1, 4, 7, 8, 10, 13, 14, 17, 18, 20–21, 22, 25, 29; Red Line Editorial, 27

Library of Congress Cataloging-in-Publication Data
Library of Congress Cataloging-in-Publication Data is available on the Library of Congress website.

ISBN
979-8-88998-028-5 (hardcover)
979-8-88998-071-1 (paperback)
979-8-88998-154-1 (ebook pdf)
979-8-88998-114-5 (hosted ebook)

Printed in the United States of America
Mankato, MN
012024

About the Author

Nick Rebman is a writer and editor who lives in Minnesota.

Table of Contents

CHAPTER 1
Sunny Summer 5

CHAPTER 2
What Is Poetry? 9

CHAPTER 3
Poetry Tools 15

Learning from Others 20

CHAPTER 4
Revising 23

Focus on Writing Poetry • 28
Glossary • 30
To Learn More • 31
Index • 32

Chapter 1

Sunny Summer

It's a beautiful summer day. The sun is shining. The birds are singing. A boy feels inspired to write a poem about it. He wants to describe the feeling of the moment.

 Being in nature is a common topic for many poets.

The boy wants his poem to create clear **images**. So, he thinks about all five senses. Next, he opens his notebook. He writes down a few ideas. For example, he wants to describe the smell of the grass. He wants to describe the sound of the breeze, too.

Sometimes you may not be able to think of anything to write about. **Prompts** can help. You can find them online.

 Some people carry notebooks with them. That lets them write whenever they have ideas.

Now it's time to start writing the poem. The boy chooses his words carefully. Each one is important. Soon, the boy is finished. He's excited to share his poem with others.

Chapter 2

What Is Poetry?

Poetry has no limits. It can be about anything. It can also take any form. Poetry often captures what an experience is like. It may create images in the reader's mind. Or it may show feelings.

Poems can describe events that aren't possible in the real world!

 Poetry's use of sound makes it similar to music.

Poets often focus on the sound and **rhythm** of their words. One way is with rhyme. That's when two words have the same ending sound. Rhyme can link words together for readers. It can also form **patterns**.

Poets can also use many tools to create rhythm. For example, meter is a pattern in the poem's **syllables**. Take the word *flower*. This word has two syllables. The first syllable is *flow*. It is stressed. That means most people say it louder.

Did You Know?

Free verse poems don't follow any form. Each line can be as short or as long as the poet wants. It depends on the mood that the poet is trying to create.

Flower's second syllable is *er.* It is unstressed. People tend to say it quieter. It gets less attention.

There are many kinds of meter. For instance, you might choose a pattern of unstressed, stressed. Here is an example. The stressed syllables are underlined.

The <u>flow</u>ers <u>bloom</u>.

The <u>blues</u> are <u>bright</u>

and <u>light</u> the <u>room</u>.

Some poems have a specific number of syllables. A haiku is one

 Poets in Japan invented haiku hundreds of years ago.

example. This type of poem has only three lines. The first line has five syllables. The second line has seven. And the third line has five.

Chapter 3

Poetry Tools

Poetry is a great way to use your imagination. Many poems create specific feelings. They can be funny or sad. They can be peaceful or angry. Poets use several tools to bring out these feelings.

 Some poets use their feelings to begin writing. Other poets start with images or phrases.

Simile and metaphor are two common tools. Both tools compare one thing to another. A simile uses the words *like* or *as*. For example, "The man is sneaky like a snake." A metaphor goes further. It says one thing *is* another thing. For instance, "The man is a snake." Similes and metaphors help create clear pictures in readers' minds.

Repetition is another tool. When words are repeated, readers are more likely to remember them.

 Snakes are sneaky, scaly, and have other features. Each feature can be used in a simile or metaphor.

Suppose you wrote, "The dancer stumbled, but she did not fall. She did not fall." The repeated words show that this idea is extra important.

 The S sound may remind readers of the sound of boiling soup.

Poets also use alliteration. That's when several nearby words begin with the same sound. For example, "Soup simmers on the stove." The

S sound makes the words feel more musical and fun.

Finally, think about where you put line breaks. Line breaks make the reader pause. So, lots of breaks will make your poem feel slower. Fewer line breaks will make it feel faster.

Poets may want to **emphasize** certain words. They often put these words at the ends of lines. That can give the words more attention.

WRITE LIKE A PRO

Learning from Others

Reading can help you become a better writer. So, read as much poetry as you can find. Look for many different styles. That's a great way to learn how other poets write. Also, be sure to read poems out loud. Listen for patterns in the sounds.

You can also copy the style of a poet you like. For instance, you might borrow the title of a famous poem. Or you might borrow the poem's first line. Over time, this can help you develop your own style.

Libraries and bookstores often have whole sections filled with poetry.

whine 2. Inf. (Inf.), grouse, moan, sigh, bitch (Sl.), grumble, establish, fix, found, set, sett with, coach, familiarize initiate, instruct, prepare, tutor

dazed, dizzy, shaky, unsteady,

groundless baseless, chimer false, idle, illusory, imaginar ized, uncalled-for, unfounded, unprovoked, unsupported, unwa

groundwork base, basis, c footing, foundation, fundamenta naries, preparation, spadework, nings

hostler or bleman ~v. primp turn out tend nu

n. 1. aggregation, ass band, batch, bunch, clique, clump, cluste mpany, congregation, action, formation, gang, ga ation, pack, party, set, troop ge, assemble, associate, assort lass, classify, dispose, gather, m er, organize, put together, range, ssociate, band together, cluster, c gate, consort, fraternize, gather, together

grouse 1. v. beef (Sl.), bellyache bitch (Sl.), carp, complain, find fault, (Inf.), grouch (Inf.), grumble, moan, w 2. n. beef (Sl.), complai tax, (Inf.)

Chapter 4

Revising

When you finish a poem, be sure to **revise** it. Look for places to use better words. That can make your images clearer. Also, read your poem out loud. Consider how you can improve its sound and rhythm.

 A thesaurus is often useful when you revise poems. It can help you find words with similar meanings.

Suppose you wrote, "The old pickup trucks make lots of noise." This line explains an idea. But it doesn't create a clear image. Also, it doesn't have much rhythm. Instead, you could write, "The pickups thunder by like rusty storms." The simile *like rusty storms* creates a

Some people take part in poetry readings. They share their poems in public.

 First drafts of poems can come quickly. But many poets spend a long time revising.

more striking image than *old*. Also, *thunder* is a specific sound. Readers can hear the noise in their minds. Finally, the line has a nice rhythm. The syllables follow a pattern.

After you revise your poem, check the spelling. In some poems, words may be misspelled. Other poems may not use **punctuation**. That's okay. But if you do these things, there should be a reason. They should create a certain feeling.

Finally, share your poem with people you trust. They can tell you what they liked. And they can explain what didn't seem clear. This feedback can help you become a better poet!

PARTS OF A POEM

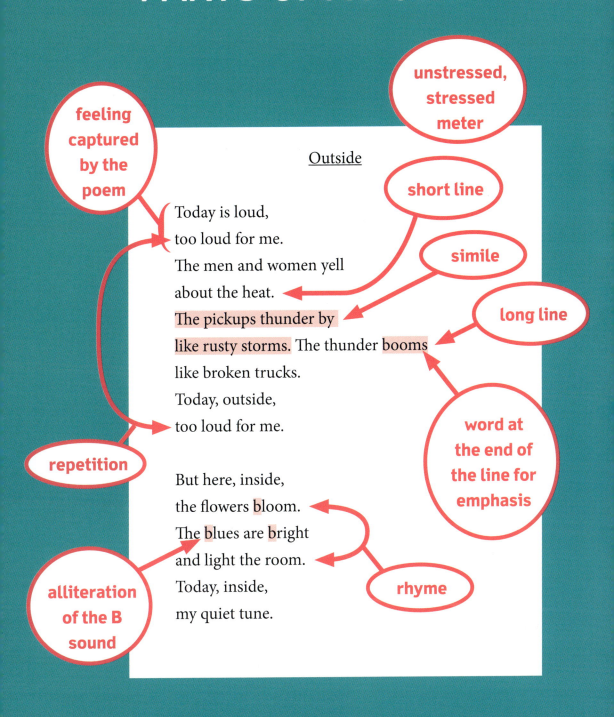

FOCUS ON
Writing Poetry

Write your answers on a separate piece of paper.

1. Write a paragraph that explains the main ideas of Chapter 3.

2. What is your favorite type of poetry? Why?

3. Which tool uses several words that begin with the same sound?
   - **A.** alliteration
   - **B.** simile
   - **C.** metaphor

4. When might repetition be most useful?
   - **A.** when you are using prompts to start writing
   - **B.** when you want the reader to remember certain words
   - **C.** when you want the poem to feel like it's moving slowly

5. What does **unstressed** mean in this book?

*Flower's second syllable is er. It is **unstressed**. People tend to say it quieter.*

    A. not nervous
    B. not part of a word
    C. not as heavy or loud

6. What does **feedback** mean in this book?

*They can tell you what they liked. And they can explain what didn't seem clear. This **feedback** can help you become a better poet!*

    A. ideas for what to change
    B. poems that do not rhyme
    C. friends who like poetry

Answer key on page 32.

Glossary

emphasize
To make something more noticeable, or to show that something is important.

images
Parts of a poem that create pictures in the reader's mind.

patterns
Things that repeat regularly.

prompts
Topics that people use to guide their writing.

punctuation
Marks used in writing to separate parts of sentences or make the meanings clear. Two examples are commas and periods.

revise
To improve a piece of writing by adding, removing, or changing details.

rhythm
In poetry, the pattern of short and long phrases and syllables to create a certain flow of sound.

syllables
Parts of a word that include vowel sounds.

To Learn More

BOOKS

Eason, Sarah, and Louise Spilsbury. *How Do I Write Well?* Shrewsbury, UK: Cheriton Children's Books, 2022.

Heinrichs, Ann. *Similes and Metaphors*. Mankato, MN: The Child's World, 2020.

Van Oosbree, Ruthie, and Lauren Kukla. *Free Verse Poems*. Minneapolis: Abdo Publishing, 2023.

NOTE TO EDUCATORS

Visit **www.focusreaders.com** to find lesson plans, activities, links, and other resources related to this title.

Index

A
alliteration, 18–19, 27

E
experiences, 9

F
feelings, 5, 9, 15, 26–27
free verse poems, 11

H
haiku, 12–13

I
images, 6, 9, 23–25

L
line breaks, 19
lines, 11, 13, 19, 20, 24–25, 27

M
metaphor, 16
meter, 11–12, 27

P
prompts, 6

R
repetition, 16–17, 27
revising, 23–26
rhyme, 10, 27
rhythm, 10–11, 23–25

S
senses, 6
simile, 16, 24–25, 27
sound, 6, 10, 18–19, 20, 23, 25, 27
syllables, 11–13, 25

W
words, 7, 10–11, 16–19, 23, 26–27

Answer Key: 1. Answers will vary; **2.** Answers will vary; **3.** A; **4.** B; **5.** C; **6.** A